Carpets and Rugs

DOLLS HOUSE DO-IT-YOURSELF

Carpets and Rugs

Sue Hawkins

David & Charles

Dedication
For Cherry

A DAVID & CHARLES BOOK

First published in the UK in 2003

Copyright © Sue Hawkins 2003

Distributed in North America
by F&W Publications, Inc.
4700 East Galbraith Road
Cincinnati, OH 45236
1-800-289-0963

A catalogue record for this book is available from the British Library.

ISBN 0 7153 1434 3 paperback

Printed in Hong Kong by Dai Nippon Printing
For David & Charles
Brunel House   Newton Abbot   Devon

Executive Editor   Cheryl Brown
Desk Editor   Jennifer Proverbs
Executive Art Editor   Ali Myer
Senior Designer   Pru Rogers
Copy-editor   Linda Clements
Production Controller   Ros Napper

Visit our website at www.davidandcharles.co.uk

David & Charles books are available from all good bookshops;
alternatively you can contact our Orderline on (0)1626 334555
or write to us at FREEPOST EX2110, David & Charles *Direct*,
Newton Abbot TQ12 4ZZ (No stamp required UK mainland).

DOLLS HOUSE DO-IT-YOURSELF

Carpets and Rugs

Contents

Introduction

I have been involved with the needlework world for many years and it has always been the small and detailed embroideries that have attracted me most. When the opportunity to work on this collection of miniature carpets and rugs was offered to me there was no hesitation, and I have thoroughly enjoyed creating them all.

From before the Christian era right up until the present day carpets and rugs have been prized as works of art and the most distinctive ones today are still based on the great weaving traditions of the past. With the designs in this book I have tried to reflect this idea, providing a selection of little treasures in a variety of styles for the one-twelfth scale

model maker. I have included designs suitable for many historical periods and styles of decoration, including Regency, Victorian, Georgian, Art Deco, Oriental and contemporary. The carpets and rugs are mostly worked in tent stitch but I have also included some other techniques. For example, there is a tiny rag rug and an embroidered felt numnah, and for those of you in a hurry why not try the bordered velvet carpet where only the outside border is stitched.

The tent stitch rugs are worked on a variety of sizes of canvas and in different colourways. I urge you to experiment with colour schemes and canvas sizes to create your own variations or even try a little designing of your own. The finer the canvas that you can work on the more accurate the scale will be, but remember that embroidery should be a pleasure and that pleasure in the making will always show in the finished piece, so do not try to work so

fine a canvas that you cannot see what you are doing. Once the embroidery is complete, turn to the section on making up carpets and rugs – stretching, edging and fringing – to decide how you should finish your little work of art.

It seems to me that dolls' houses are very personal and that the things that are handmade with loving care rather than purchased as finished items have a charm all their own and must give more pleasure to the owner. They are, after all, unique. In many ways, dolls' houses are just like full-sized houses: some are furnished to reflect a specific historical period with not a thing out of place and with amazing attention to detail, while others are a jumble of all the things that the owner takes a fancy to. Whichever type your dolls' house is I hope that there will be some carpet and rug designs here that will make you run to find your needle and threads.

Materials and Equipment

This section contains useful, illustrated information on the basic materials and equipment you will need to stitch the carpets and rugs as shown in this book.

Embroidery Fabrics

Canvas This is available in various mesh sizes. All the designs in this book can be worked on any size provided that you can see what you are doing – don't forget that embroidery should be a pleasure so do not punish yourself by trying to work too fine a canvas. Many of the projects use an 18 count canvas, that is, 18 threads to the inch. The best canvas to use is interlock mono canvas, where the threads along the length are in fact double threads twisted together to hold the cross threads firmly in place. This produces a more stable canvas, ideal for carpets as the edges can be cut away right up to the stitching. The finer canvases are not available as interlock so when using 22 or 24 threads to the inch, the edges need turning back and sewing in place rather than cutting away (described on page 13).

When cutting canvas or linen for a project, add at least 6in (15cm) so there is about 2–3in (5–7.5cm) of bare fabric around the finished piece. On smaller rugs 4in (10cm) extra will suffice.

Linen Linen is an evenweave fabric normally used for counted cross stitch but which is very suitable for miniature carpets and rugs as it produces a softer result, particularly for stair carpets where flexibility is needed. Four projects are worked on linen, on 26, 28 and 36 counts.

Felt Felt was used for the embroidered numnah on page 58 to create an authentic look to the rug. Felt is available commercially in many colours, though it can be great fun to gather your own wool from the hedgerows and make your own.

General Equipment

If you are already interested in needlework you will undoubtedly have a collection of tools and accessories, some essential and some just because you like them! The basics you will need are described below. See page 12 for the materials and equipment needed for stretching carpets and rugs.

Scissors A pair of sharp scissors for cutting fabric will be needed, plus a small sharp pair of embroidery scissors for cutting threads. You will also need an unpicker in the event of stitching mistakes.

Embroidery frames It is better, but not essential, to use a frame when stitching carpets to keep work stable (however you will still need to stretch the finished carpet – see page 12 for step-by-step instructions showing how to do this).

There are many types of frame available so choose one that you are most comfortable with. Follow the manufacturer's instructions for mounting the canvas. Never use an embroidery hoop on canvas unless you have one big enough to contain the entire worked area, as the canvas will become distorted between the rings and if this distortion is stitched over there will be a shadow in the embroidery which often remains, even after careful stretching.

Magnifiers Do not struggle with your eyesight – buy a magnifier if you have difficulty. There are many different types available: some sit on your chest, some clip on to your glasses and some are fixed to a stand with integral lighting. Find the one that suits you best, perhaps taking some embroidery to the shop to try it before you purchase. Daylight simulation bulbs are also helpful, especially when stitching with pastel shades at night.

Thread organizers There are various systems to organize and hold threads that you are working with. If you are planning to design your own rugs or change some of the colours used in the projects, then manufacturers' colour charts are invaluable – ask at your local needlework shop.

Masking tape This is useful for edging the canvas to prevent threads snagging but do not buy the three-day variety – it is designed not to stick too well!

Fray Check This is a transparent fabric glue to seal fabric edges and prevent fraying – invaluable if you are not using interlock canvas or if you have a corner that looks a bit suspect. Do not worry if it seems to darken colours when you apply it as it becomes transparent as it dries. If you are in any doubt try it on spare thread before you use it on your precious stitching.

Crochet hook A small hook will be needed to pull fabric strips through canvas if you are making a hooked rag rug, such as the sunflower one on page 50.

Fabric markers These are essential for marking designs on fabric and will be needed for the sunflower rag rug and the embroidered felt numnah. Vanishing embroidery markers are perhaps the easiest to use, though the marks made will fade in a few hours. Use a water-soluble pen if the design needs to stay in place for longer, rinsing your work in water when finished to remove the pen marks.

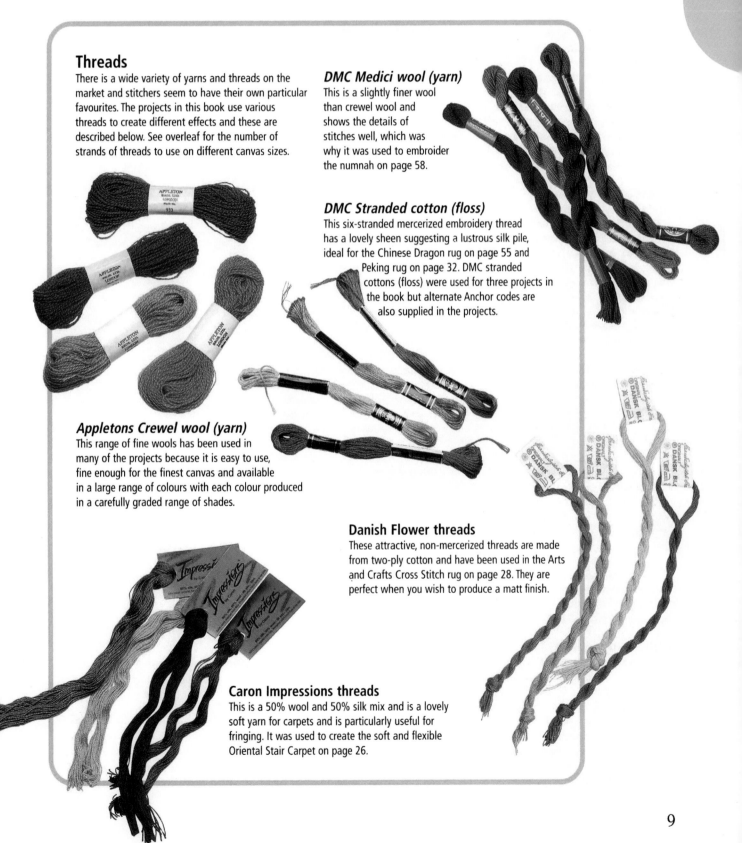

Needles

Tapestry needles It is best to use these when working on canvas as they are blunt and pass through without catching. The size required will vary according to the number of strands and the gauge of canvas being used. The threaded needle should pass easily through the canvas. As you stitch, move the needle along the thread to stop it wearing in one place. Drop the needle every now and again and let it hang freely to allow the thread to untwist. Do treat yourself to a gold-plated needle for canvaswork: it will never tarnish and remain beautifully smooth and a pleasure to use.

Crewel needles A crewel needle has been used for the embroidered numnah as it is more pointed than a tapestry needle and will pass through the felt more easily.

Threads

There is a wide variety of yarns and threads on the market and stitchers seem to have their own particular favourites. The projects in this book use various threads to create different effects and these are described below. See overleaf for the number of strands of threads to use on different canvas sizes.

DMC Medici wool (yarn)
This is a slightly finer wool than crewel wool and shows the details of stitches well, which was why it was used to embroider the numnah on page 58.

DMC Stranded cotton (floss)
This six-stranded mercerized embroidery thread has a lovely sheen suggesting a lustrous silk pile, ideal for the Chinese Dragon rug on page 55 and Peking rug on page 32. DMC stranded cottons (floss) were used for three projects in the book but alternate Anchor codes are also supplied in the projects.

Appletons Crewel wool (yarn)
This range of fine wools has been used in many of the projects because it is easy to use, fine enough for the finest canvas and available in a large range of colours with each colour produced in a carefully graded range of shades.

Danish Flower threads
These attractive, non-mercerized threads are made from two-ply cotton and have been used in the Arts and Crafts Cross Stitch rug on page 28. They are perfect when you wish to produce a matt finish.

Caron Impressions threads
This is a 50% wool and 50% silk mix and is a lovely soft yarn for carpets and is particularly useful for fringing. It was used to create the soft and flexible Oriental Stair Carpet on page 26.

Basic Techniques

The following information will help you produce perfect results, describing how to use the charts, work the stitches and finish your carpets and rugs beautifully.

Using the Charts

Most of the carpets and rugs are stitched from colour charts with symbols to distinguish colours close in shade. One square on the chart represents one stitch on the canvas. Arrows at the sides of the charts make finding the centre easy – it is best to start there to avoid working off centre or even off the edge of the canvas. Work the design first, stitching in areas of colour, then fill in backgrounds.

Calculating Finished Sizes

Finished sizes are given for all the designs but if you want to change the canvas mesh size it will alter the size of your finished piece. To calculate the finished size of any design you need to know the stitch counts, that is the total number of chart squares across a design, both ways. Divide these counts by the count per inch of the canvas you want to use and this will give the dimensions of the carpet. Two examples are shown below.

How to calculate finished sizes

Example:
If the stitch count is 108 x 72 on an 18 count canvas;
$108 \div 18 = 6$
$72 \div 18 = 4$
Therefore the finished size is 6in x 4in.
(To change to metric, multiply by 2.5 i.e. 15 x 10cm.)

Example:
If the stitch count is 108 x 72 on a 24 count canvas;
$108 \div 24 = 4.5$
$72 \div 24 = 3$
Therefore the finished size is 4½in x 3in.
(To change to metric, multiply by 2.5 i.e. 11.25 x 7.5cm.)

How Many Strands?

Each project gives the number of strands of thread needed. The number of strands used will vary according to thread thickness, canvas size and the effect you want to achieve. Too few strands and the base fabric will show through; too many and it will be difficult to pull the thread through the fabric and produce clumsy-looking work. The table, right, gives general advice on the number of strands to use.

Starting and Finishing

To produce the best results it is advisable to start and finish your stitching neatly. There are two methods of starting: a looped start and a waste knot start. A looped start can only be used with an even number of threads, whereas a waste knot start can use any number of threads.

Loop start

To begin with a loop start with two strands, take a single thread that is twice the length that you need, fold it in half and thread the two ends through the needle leaving the loop at the other end. Push the needle up through the fabric with the first stitch and down again, leaving the loop hanging at the back. Now pass the needle through the loop and pull, anchoring the thread.

Waste knot start

To begin with a waste knot, start by knotting the end of the thread and pulling it through your canvas about 1in (2.5cm) from where you intend to begin stitching, leaving the knot on the top. Work your stitches towards the knot, catching the starting thread into the back of the stitches. When you reach the knot cut it off.

Finishing off neatly

To finish off your stitching neatly, run the thread under a few stitches on the back and snip off the thread. Do this carefully so that you do not alter the tension of the existing stitches on the front of the canvas. To begin a new length of thread or a new colour, run the thread under a few stitches on the back before you begin to stitch. Do not run a dark colour through lighter stitches as it may show through on the front.

Loop start

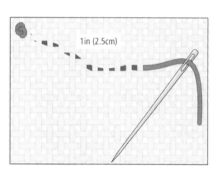
Waste knot start

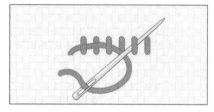
Finishing off neatly

Number of threads for different canvas sizes

Canvas size	Appletons crewel wool	Stranded cotton	Caron Impressions thread
18	2	6	2
22	1	4	1
24	1	3	1

Working the Stitches

Back stitch

This is often worked with tent stitch to enhance the details of a design. Always work the design and any surrounding background before the outlining – it will not show unless it sits on top of the tent stitch. Back stitch is shown on the charts by solid straight lines. Following the diagram, bring the needle up at 1, down at 2, up at 3, back down at 1 and so on.

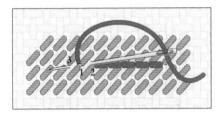

Chain stitch

This attractive stitch has been used in the felt numnah. Follow the diagram, bringing the needle up through the fabric at 1. Go down at 2, forming a loop of thread and bring the needle up in the loop at 3. Pull the thread gently to make the first loop of the chain. Repeat to work the whole chain. Do not pull the thread too tightly, allowing the loops to remain rounded. To finish the chain, catch down the last loop with a small stitch.

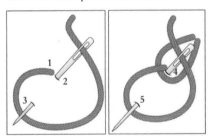

Cross stitch

This is a commonly used stitch in embroidery and has been used in the Arts and Crafts rug. Follow the diagram, starting at the bottom left corner and crossing diagonally to top right. Bring the needle back up at the bottom right corner and cross to the top left corner to complete the stitch. For neater stitching, work all top stitches in the same direction.

Herringbone stitch

This versatile stitch has been used to hold back the edges of carpets and rugs worked on linen or non-interlock canvas. Follow the numbering on the diagram to work the stitch and when making the upper part of the stitch, work through the turned-over edge and into the back of the embroidery to make it firmer.

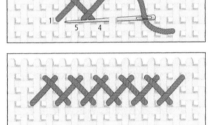

Long-legged cross stitch

This stitch produces a braided effect that is very useful for edging carpets and rugs. It is usually worked over two canvas threads but in order to make a tight, close edge, work over one thread only (see diagram). As the stitch is so close, use half the number of strands that you used for the stitching. So if your rug used two strands on 18 count canvas, work the edge in one strand. If you worked in one strand, then use one for the edging as well.

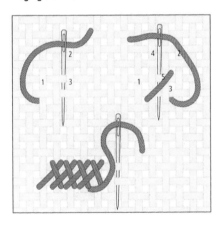

Tent stitch

Most of the projects are worked using tent stitch. There are two methods: continental and diagonal. Diagonal tent stitch (basketweave stitch) distorts the canvas less, especially when working backgrounds. Continental tent stitch is easier to work when stitching individual motifs and irregular shaped parts of a design.

diagonal tent stitch

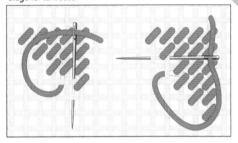

continental tent stitch

Velvet stitch

This stitch has been used in the front door mats to create a long, dense pile. Follow the diagram, working from left to right in rows and from the bottom to the top. After all the rows have been worked cut the loops and trim to the desired length.

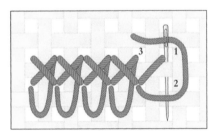
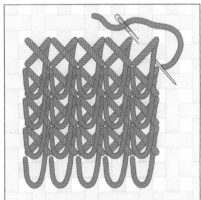

Making Up Carpets and Rugs

This section provides valuable advice on finishing your carpets and rugs beautifully – explaining how to stretch the stitched canvas, edge it neatly and add attractive fringes.

Stretching and Starching

It is in the nature of canvaswork to distort as it is worked, particularly when using tent stitch. Even if you have used a frame and you think your embroidery is square you should still stretch and starch it – you will be surprised how much the appearance is improved. Not only will the piece be perfectly square but the tension of the stitching will become more even. If you are tempted to miss out this vital stage between the stitching and the finishing your carpet will never look as good as it might. Carpets and rugs worked on linen will not need stretching but should be carefully steam pressed on the wrong side. The edges will need to be trimmed, turned to the back and secured with herringbone stitch (see Edging page 13).

1 Start by covering the board with the sheet of squared paper and secure with masking tape around the edges.

2 Place the embroidery right side down on top of the squared paper. You will be able to see the squares of the paper through the unstitched margin of the canvas. Following the line on the paper, begin nailing in one corner about 2in (5cm) away from the embroidery – hammer the nails in just far enough to hold firmly in the board. Follow one line of holes in the canvas and nail into every second intersection of a line on the paper. It is important to keep the nails no more than ¾in (2cm) apart or the edge of the carpet will not be straight. When you have completed the first side, go back to the corner and repeat for the side at right angles to it.

3 Draw a pencil line from the last nail on each side, crossing to the corner diagonally opposite the one you started from. Lift the canvas and using the squares on the paper find the position on the paper where the lines cross from the nailed corner; this is where the last corner of the canvas must be stretched to. Pull out the embroidery, nail the last corner and finish nailing the last two sides (see

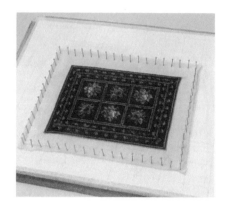

picture above). If your work is badly distorted it will help to dampen the embroidery at this stage. If you really struggle then blow steam from your iron on to the canvas to soften it.

4 Mix a small quantity of starch paste to the consistency of soft butter and, using the palette knife, spread it evenly but sparingly over the back of the embroidery (as shown below). Try not to let the starch go over the edges of the embroidery as it will stick to the paper and spoil the board for future use. Allow to dry naturally and completely. Remove all the nails when finished. Your carpet is now ready for edging.

You will need

Large, flat clean board
(chipboard is ideal)

Sheet of dressmaker's paper
(marked in 1cm squares)

Plenty of clean 1in (2.5cm) nails and
a small hammer.

Cold water starch e.g. wallpaper paste –
buy a brand without plasticizer

Masking tape

Hard pencil

Small kitchen palette knife (one with a
rubber blade is ideal)

Edging

Generally, smaller rugs look good with a fringe at the ends while carpets are better just edged all the way around. All the carpets and rugs in this book are edged in long-legged cross stitch over one thread – see page 11.

1 Work long-legged cross stitch over one thread along the two long straight edges of the rug. Pull the stitches tightly as you go and you will find that the edge seems to turn over of its own accord.

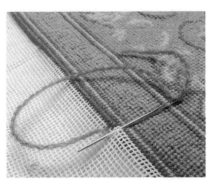

2 If you have worked on interlock canvas you can cut away against the stitched edge – the canvas will not fray as the threads are locked together. A finer canvas or linen it is unlikely to be interlocked so trim to within ⅜in (1cm) of the edge, fold the unstitched edge to the back and hold it down with herringbone stitch (page 11). You could seal this edge with Fray Check before you stitch it down.

Fringing

All rug fringes are worked in Caron Impressions colour 1146. This is just the right colour to imitate full-sized warp threads. The soft thread lies fairly flat whereas pure wool tends to make a rather full, springy fringe. Use two strands on 18 count canvas and one strand on 22 or 24 count.

The fringes on the larger rugs have a tent stitch border in cream, like the woven edge of a full-sized rug (described below). The smaller ones have the fringe worked right up against the stitching, with the canvas folded to the back and held down with herringbone stitch. Where the fringe sits right up against the stitching you may see a little canvas showing through, so fill this gap with a row of back stitch in the same thread as the fringe.

1 To work a fringe, begin at one end of one short side of the rug, leaving loops between each stitch. Work three canvas threads away from the stitching, as in the picture. When you reach the end of the thread join in another, leaving the ends hanging.

2 Once you have worked all across one end, fold the canvas so that the fringe is on the edge. Line up the holes so that you can work tent stitch through both layers to hold the edge together. Begin with a row that is nearest to the fringe leaving a row next to the rug stitching.

3 When you reach the other side of the rug oversew the cut edge and then work tent stitch back along the row next to the rug stitching. When this row is complete, oversew the first edge and finish off your thread.

4 Turn over to the back of the rug and cut away the bare canvas carefully.

5 Cut the fringe loops and trim to the right length. Open up the twists of each thread of the fringe by running a needle along the length of each one to make the fringe finer.

Regency Roses Carpet

This attractive Regency-style carpet design in soft pastel colours is very versatile as both the colouring and size can be altered to suit your dolls' house décor. To change the colourway, keep the groups of colours the same – there are four corals, two greens, two golds and two blues – changing any of these to tone with existing wallpaper or furniture.

The carpet is quite large but could easily be made smaller by omitting the outer rose border, finishing at the inner blue border. Conversely, you could stitch just the outer border and then use a velvet rectangle to fill the central area (see the Bordered Velvet Carpet on page 22). You could also work just the central medallion as an oval hearth rug.

You will need

18 x 16in (46 x 40cm) 18 count interlock canvas

Size 22 tapestry needle

Appletons crewel wool (yarn) as follows:
One skein: dark coral 205; mid coral 204; light coral 203; very light coral 202; dark green 334; light green 332; gold 693; dark blue 154
Two skeins: light blue 152
Three skeins: light gold 692

1 Start by binding the edges of the canvas with masking tape to prevent threads snagging. Fold the canvas in four to find the centre and mark the folds with a hard pencil or fabric pen.

2 Using two strands of crewel wool (yarn), work the design from the chart overleaf, using continental tent stitch for the design and diagonal tent stitch (page 11) for the backgrounds. Begin with the central medallion, working the roses first followed by the blue spots and border and then filling in the gold background. When working the blue spots diagonally up and down, allow the thread to trail across the back of the canvas. Once the gold background is stitched this will cover the blue threads.

3 Count carefully out to the next border and complete the inner area. Finally, work the rose border and the blue outer border.

4 Complete your carpet by referring to page 12 for starching and stretching and to page 13 for edging.

The design of this carpet is typical of Georgian and Regency periods. Trade suddenly flourished during these times as the wealthy were able to travel more easily and bring back treasured textiles to their grand houses. A carpet of this type would probably have been made in Europe and would grace a formal drawing room or maybe the master's study.

Stitch count 219 x 171
Finished size 12 x 9½in (31 x 24cm)
Carpet shown smaller than actual size

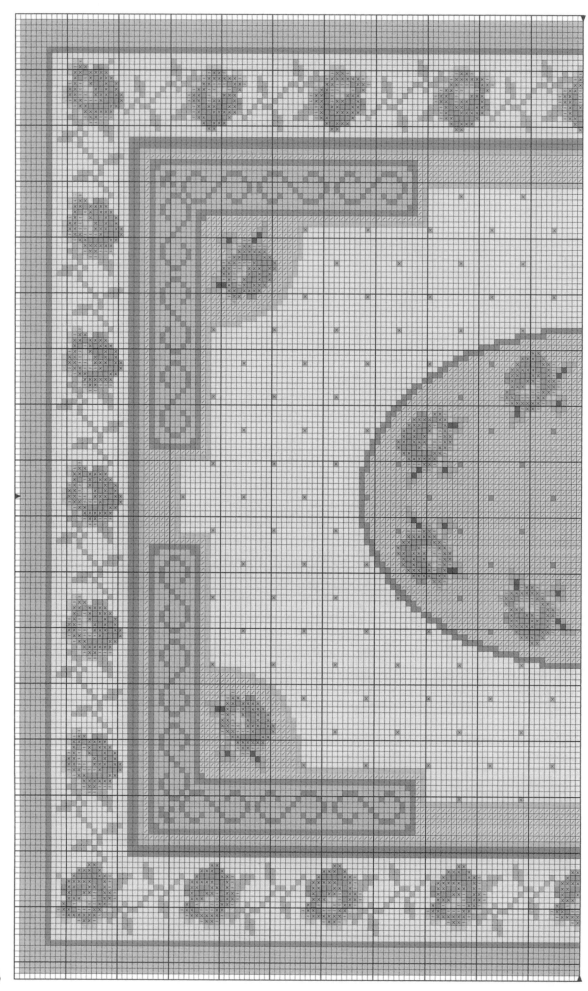

16

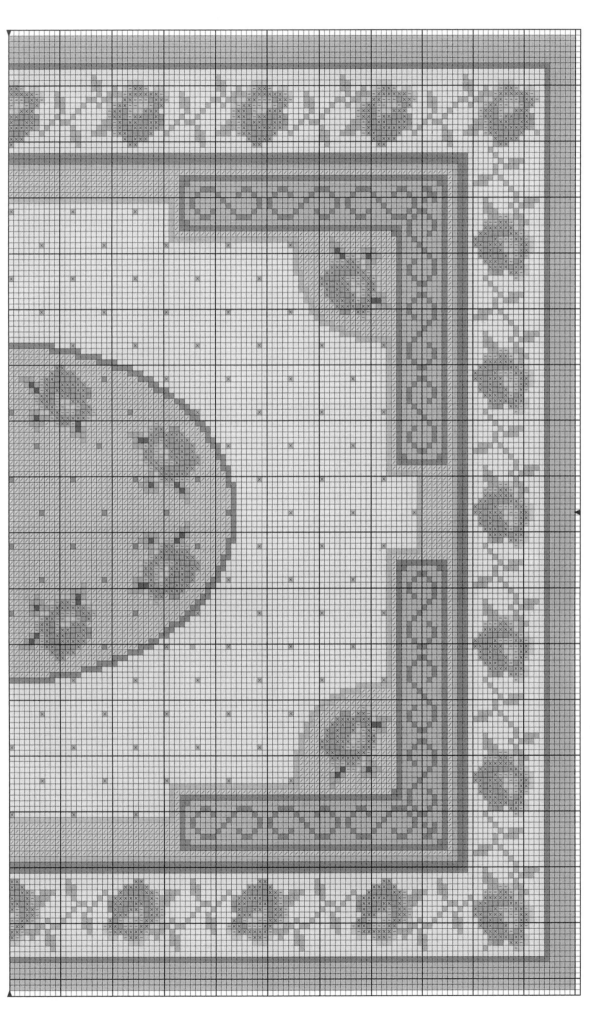

Regency Roses Carpet

Appletons crewel wool

	152
	154
/	693
	692
	332
	334
	202
−	203
✕	204
	205

Victorian Squares

This typically Victorian-style carpet is worked with a charcoal background but if you prefer this could be changed to cream or a pastel shade to suit your dolls' house. Each square is a complete design so you could make cushions to match the carpet from single squares or a rug from four squares or even an oblong hearth rug using just two.

You will need

16 x 14in (40 x 36cm) 18 count interlock canvas

Size 22 tapestry needle

Appletons crewel wool (yarn) as follows:
One skein: dark rose pink 757; mid rose pink 755; light rose pink 754; very light rose pink 752; dark green 336; mid green 334; light green 332; dark blue green 298; mid blue green 295; light blue green 293; dark mauve 606; light mauve 604
Two skeins: very dark rose pink 759; gold 695
Seven skeins: charcoal 998 for background

1 Start by binding the edges of the canvas with masking tape to prevent threads snagging. Fold the canvas in four to find the centre and mark the folds with a hard pencil or fabric pen.

2 Using two strands of crewel wool (yarn), work the design from the chart overleaf, using continental tent stitch for the design and diagonal tent stitch (page 11) for the background. Begin with the border lines between the squares, go on to work the flowers in each square and then fill in the backgrounds to the squares.

3 Now work the ribbon and flower border and the outer border and finally fill in the border background.

4 Complete your rug by referring to page 12 for starching and stretching and to page 13 for edging.

In the mid 19th century canvaswork became very popular. The designs were worked from hand-painted charts produced in Berlin in Germany and later in Britain. There were thousands of charts available but they were all very similar in style, with animals, birds and flowers in abundance. The wools used were very bright in colour and were dyed in Berlin, and the name 'Berlin woolwork' became synonymous with Victorian canvaswork. The lady stitchers were prolific and many examples exist today and these, along with the charts themselves, are very collectable.

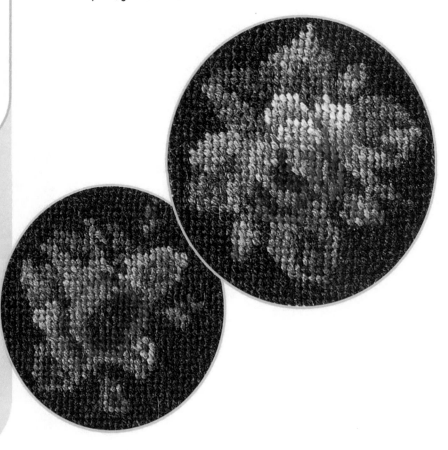

Stitch count 188 x 146
Finished size 10⅜ x 8⅛in (26.5 x 20.6cm)
Rug shown smaller than actual size

Victorian Squares

Appletons crewel wool

	759
+	757
−	755
	754
	752
	695
	336
	334
	332
	298
•	295
	293
	606
	604
	998

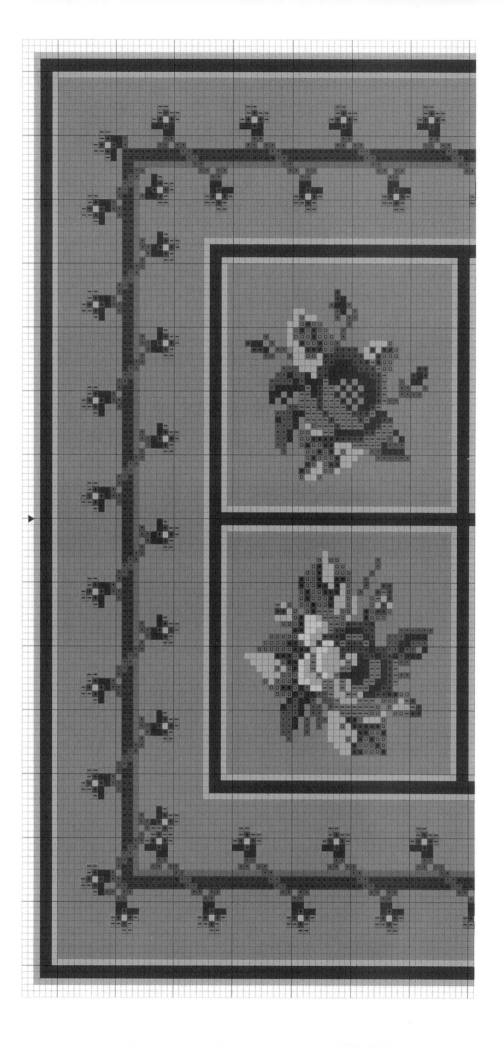

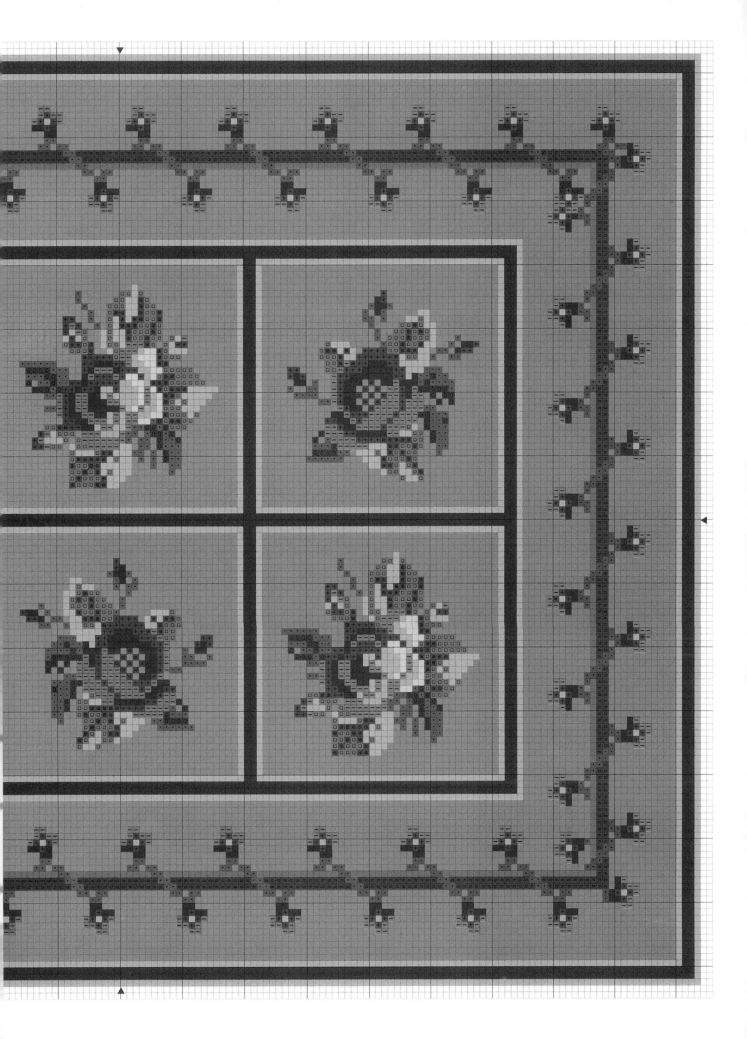

Bordered Velvet Carpet

Here is a way of cheating with a large stitched carpet – the border is stitched but the central area is velvet! You will probably find it easier to choose the colour of the velvet first and then match the background colour of the border to it. Cotton velvet is a better choice as it is not as shiny as a synthetic one and will not fray at the edge as easily. The size of the carpet can be altered to suit your room and if changing the size you will find it helpful to draw the corners on some squared paper before you begin to stitch. Some alternative borders are shown on the chart but you could also use borders from many of the other rugs in this book.

You will need

16 x 16in (40 x 40cm) 18 count
interlock canvas

Size 22 tapestry needle

Appletons crewel wool (yarn) as follows:
One skein: dark coral 207;
light coral 205; dark green 334;
light green 332; gold 694
Five skeins: charcoal 202 for background

10 x 10in (25 x 25cm) velvet

Tailor's chalk

Clear multi-purpose adhesive

This simple flower and trellis border used for this carpet will sit happily in most styles of dolls' house. It will be useful in the bedrooms where you might want to spend less time on a detailed carpet especially when large areas are covered by the bed.

1 Start by binding the edges of the canvas with masking tape to prevent snagging. As the centre of this carpet is not stitched it is easier to start the stitching at one corner. Allow 3in (7.5cm) of unstitched canvas around the design. Measure in 3in (7.5cm) from each side on one corner and begin with the outer border here.

2 Using two strands of crewel wool (yarn), work the design from the chart overleaf, using continental tent stitch for the design and diagonal tent stitch (page 11) for the background. Begin with the border lines, the flowers and the trellis and then fill in the background.

3 You will need to stretch the canvas as though it is all stitched, as the inner area will probably have distorted a little. Starch the back of the stitched border but not the bare canvas and refer to page 12

for stretching. Once the canvas is stretched, finish the outer edges with long-legged cross stitch as described on page 11.

4 To attach the central velvet part to the canvas, lay the velvet flat on a table with the canvas over it. You will be able to see through the canvas to mark the positions of the inner corners with pins. Remove the canvas and join up the pins with tailor's chalk lines on the velvet. Now cut out the velvet. Apply adhesive to the bare canvas and carefully lay the velvet in place. Place the carpet face down on a table and cover with heavy books until the glue is dry.

Stitch count 187 x 187
Finished size 10⅜ x 10⅜in (26.4 x 26.4cm)
Carpet shown smaller than actual size

Bordered Velvet Carpet

Appletons crewel wool

 334

 332

205

694

207

202

Alternative borders

692

903

905

925

934

Front Door Mats

Don't be misled by the tiny size of these mats: because each loop in the pile is made up of three stitches there are actually over three thousand stitches in each mat! You could substitute ordinary tent stitch for the velvet stitch but the effect of the cut pile is very realistic. Instructions are given for creating the footprints mat but also charted are two alternatives: one for a sun ray door mat and a cream design with a blue twist border, which if worked in soft stranded cotton (floss) would make a perfect bathroom mat.

Mat shown actual size

1 Start by binding the edges of the canvas with masking tape. Work the mat in velvet stitch (page 11) using one strand of crewel wool (yarn). You will need to work the velvet stitch in rows from left to right and from the bottom upwards because of the way that the loops are formed in this stitch, otherwise you will not be able to see what you are doing. It is easy to work out roughly where to begin as this is such a small piece.

2 For the footprints mat, work the bottom row in brown and then the next row in grey except for the first and last stitch. You will find that you can carry a thread up each side of the mat to work the border. As you reach the footprints continue working in rows introducing a thread for each one – you can thread this back through the back of the grey stitches and then pick it up again on the next row. Continue in this way until you reach the top row. Do not cut any loops to make the pile until you have edged your mat.

3 To complete your mat, refer to page 12 for stretching and page 13 for edging.

You will need

6 x 5in (15 x 12cm) 18 count interlock canvas for each mat

Size 22 tapestry needle

Appletons crewel wool (yarn) as follows (use one skein of each):
Footprint mat
brown 903; grey 965
Sun ray mat
brown 903; dark brown 904
Blue twist mat
white 991; light blue 563; dark blue 565

Stitch counts Footprints 40 x 27, Sun Ray 41 x 27
Finished size 2¼in x 1½in (5.6 x 3.8cm)

Stitch count Blue Twist 40 x 27
Finished size 2¼in x 1¾in (5.6 x 4.5cm)

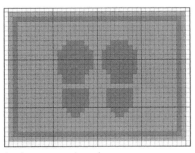

Appletons crewel wool

■ 903
■ 965

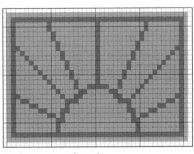

Appletons crewel wool

■ 903
■ 904

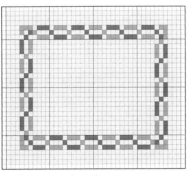

Appletons crewel wool

□ 991
■ 563
■ 565

Oriental Stair Carpet

This stair carpet is worked on linen rather than canvas to produce a softer finish that is easier to fold over stair treads. This, combined with the very soft Caron thread, a mix of wool and silk, makes a fairly thin carpet which is more in scale than a thicker canvas one would be. However, if time or your eyesight prohibits working on such a fine gauge, use an 18 or 22 count canvas and omit the red borders to make the carpet narrow enough.

If your staircase has stair rods, fitting the carpet is easy; just stitch it to the required length, finish the edges and allow some unstitched linen at each end to wrap over the ends of the stairs, to be glued down out of sight (alternatively, use very fine Velcro). If the stairs are fixed in the dolls' house then fold back the unstitched linen and glue the top and bottom to the treads. To calculate the total length of a staircase, use a tape measure to measure the vertical and horizontal parts of all the steps.

You will need

6in (15cm) wide x the length of your stairs plus 6in (15cm) 26 count evenweave linen

Size 24 tapestry needle

Caron Impressions thread as follows:
One skein: green 5002; yellow 4012; blue 0076; purple 6021; red 3061; cream 1146
(Note: To make a longer length double up on purple, red, blue and cream)

1 Bind the edges of the linen with masking tape or oversew it to prevent fraying. Fold the fabric in half lengthways to find the centre line and mark the fold with a hard pencil or fabric pen.

2 Stitch the design from the chart, starting work 3in (7.5cm) from one end of your fabric. Work over one thread of linen using one strand of Caron Impressions, using continental tent stitch for the purple outlines and diagonal tent stitch (page 11) for the filling colours. Begin with the purple outlines and then fill in the shapes with the appropriate colours as you go. The chart can be repeated as many times as you like.

3 To complete your stair carpet, refer to page 12 for stretching and to page 13 for edging.

This design is taken from the borders of a Kazak carpet woven in the 19th century. It makes a striking stair carpet but would also be lovely as a runner along a hallway or landing. The strong colours look best with dark wood.

Caron Impressions

■ 5002
■ 4012
■ 0076
■ 6021
■ 3061
□ 1146

Stitch count 44 wide x as long as you need
Finished size 1¾in (4.3cm) wide
Carpet shown wider than actual size

Arts and Crafts Cross Stitch Rug

Danish Flower threads and cross stitch have been used for this pretty William Morris-style rug. Many cross stitch rugs were worked on canvas using wool (yarn), but for the dolls' house scale there are few wools fine enough. The matt finish of Flower threads is preferable to mercerized cotton, which would have been too shiny. If you prefer you could use canvas and work in wool (yarn) and tent stitch.

You will need

14 x 12in (35.5 x 30cm) 36 count
evenweave linen

Size 26 tapestry needle

Danish Flower threads as follows:
One skein: dark blue green 9;
mid blue green 224; light blue green 231;
dark green 206; light green 10;
dark pink 96; mid pink 12;
light pink 113; dark gold 54;
light gold 46
Four skeins: deep blue 220

1 Begin by binding the edges of the linen with masking tape or oversewing it to prevent fraying. Fold the fabric piece in four to find the centre and mark the folds with a hard pencil or fabric pen.

2 Work the design from the chart overleaf, using cross stitch (page 11) worked over two threads of linen with one strand of Flower thread. Begin with the central flower and work outwards to complete the flowers, pomegranates, leaves and curling stems.

3 Work the inner dark gold border line and then the leaf border and outer light gold edging. Finish by stitching all the background in deep blue.

4 To complete your rug, refer to page 13 for edging instructions.

William Morris designs are familiar to most of us and many are still used on fabrics by Liberty of London. This design is based on his work in the late 19th century. Designs were less formal than previously and flowing floral motifs abounded. This rug has a central floral motif with pomegranates and a curling leaf border. Use it under an oak table and dining chairs and the warm colours will offset the wood beautifully.

Stitch count 140 x 100
Finished size 7¾ x 5½in (19.8 x 14cm)
Rug shown actual size

Arts and Crafts Cross Stitch Rug

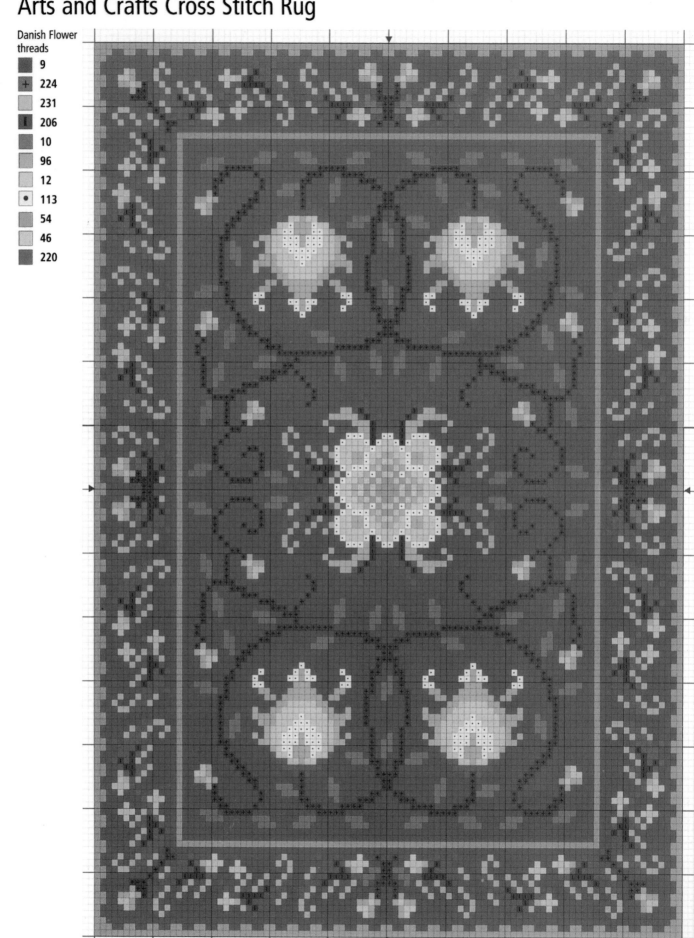

Danish Flower threads

■	9
+	224
■	231
▮	206
■	10
■	96
■	12
•	113
■	54
■	46
■	220

Bedside Rug

This simple but useful little rug could be placed in many other rooms in a dolls' house as well as by a bedside and the unobtrusive pattern will sit happily in many periods and styles. As it is worked in only two colours, it is really easy to change them to complement your colour schemes. It has been worked on fine 22 count canvas but will look just as good on an 18 count, in which case you should use two strands of crewel wool (yarn).

You will need

8 x 7in (20 x 18cm) 22 count canvas

Size 24 tapestry needle

Appletons crewel wool (yarn) as follows:
One skein: blue 922; gold 693

Stitch count 71 x 57
Finished size 3¼ x 2½in (8 x 6.5cm)
Rug shown larger than actual size

1 Bind the edges of the canvas with masking tape to prevent snagging. Fold the canvas in four to find the centre and mark the folds with a hard pencil or fabric pen.

2 Using one strand of crewel wool (yarn) work from the chart using continental tent stitch for the design and diagonal tent stitch (page 11) for the background. Begin in the centre, stitching the gold areas of the design, then go on to stitch the blue background.

3 To complete your rug, refer to page 12 for starching and stretching and to page 13 for edging and fringing.

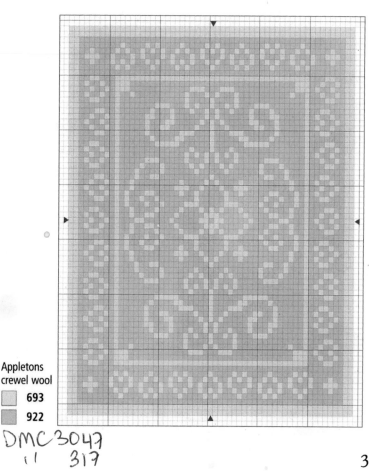

Appletons
crewel wool

	693
	922

DMC 3047
317

Peking Rug

Full-sized Peking rugs are woven in silk and are usually of extremely high quality. This miniature version is worked in stranded cotton (floss) so that the lustre of the thread gives the impression of silk. Give your rug even more sheen by separating the strands before you stitch. You could change the colouring but Chinese rugs are traditionally blue and cream and the lighter blue line of the border gives the illusion of a deep, luxurious pile. The rug was worked in DMC stranded cotton (floss) but alternative Anchor codes are also given.

You will need

14 x 11in (35 x 28cm) 18 count
interlock canvas

Size 22 tapestry needle

DMC stranded cotton (floss) as follows
(Anchor conversions in brackets):
One skein: light blue 336 (150)
Five skeins: cream 677 (802)
Six skeins: dark navy 939 (152)

1 Start by binding the edges of the canvas with masking tape to prevent threads snagging. Fold the canvas in four to find the centre and mark the folds with a hard pencil or fabric pen.

2 Use all six strands of stranded cotton (floss) for all the stitching. For a really smooth finish separate the strands and recombine them to remove the twist. Work the design from the chart overleaf, using continental tent stitch for the design and diagonal tent stitch (page 11) for the background. Begin with the central medallion.

3 Count carefully out to the border and work the light blue line, then stitch the inner background. Work the border and the navy background and finally the light blue outer line.

4 To complete your rug refer to page 12 for starching and stretching and to page 13 for edging and fringing.

Peking rugs date from the Ch'ing (Qing) dynasty (1644–1911), and as this is such a long time span this rug can be used with many style periods. The large central medallion is a *shou*, a Chinese calligraphy character. The smaller *shou* and *fou* characters in the border are symbols of longevity and happiness.

Stitch count 133 x 93
Finished size 7⅜ x 5⅛in (18.8 x 13.1cm)
Rug shown actual size

Peking Rug

DMC stranded cotton (Anchor conversions)

- ■ 939 (152)
- ☐ 677 (802)
- ▨ 336 (150)

Florentine Mat

This simple little mat can be worked in any colours of your choice and as the straight-stitched pattern is a repeating one it could be made much larger. Because it is worked over four threads, it is easy and quick to make and because it uses soft linen it needs no stretching. The mat will fill plenty of odd places all around a dolls' house, by the bath or even in front of the loo!

You will need

5 x 5in (12.5 x 12.5cm) 28 count linen

Size 24 tapestry needle

Appletons crewel wool (yarn) as follows:
One skein: blue 922; gold 693;
pink 204; cream 882

Florentine embroidery or bargello is the general name applied to needlepoint designs worked in straight stitch. The technique is named after the historical examples of this beautiful work on display at the Bargello Palace in Florence, Italy.

1 Bind the edges of the linen with masking tape or oversew it to prevent fraying. Fold the fabric in four to find the centre and mark with a hard pencil or a fabric pen.

2 Start from the centre of the chart, using one strand of crewel wool (yarn). Work the design in straight stitch with each stitch over four threads of the linen.

Finished size 2¾ x 1¾in (5.5 x 4.5cm)
Rug shown larger than actual size

3 When you have worked all the coloured shapes, fill the background with cream following the pattern of stitches already set in the colours, referring to the picture. Finally, work back stitch lines around the border in gold.

4 To complete your mat, turn the unworked linen edges over and edge with long-legged cross stitch (see page 11).

Appletons crewel wool
- 922
- 204
- 693

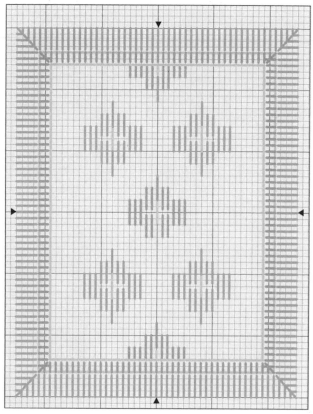

Greek-style Georgian Rug

During the Georgian period travel for pleasure became easier and very fashionable; money was plentiful for the upper classes and the style was 'elegance'. Trade flourished and there were many influences from abroad.

This beautiful rug is worked in blue and gold and because there are only three shades of gold and the background is blue, it would be very easy to change the colours. You could use three shades of soft green on a pale coral background for example.

You will need

13 x 11in (33 x 28cm) 18 count interlock canvas

Size 22 tapestry needle

Appletons crewel wool (yarn) as follows:
One skein: dark gold 696; mid gold 695; light gold 693; blue 922

1 Start by binding the edges of the canvas with masking tape to prevent threads snagging. Fold the canvas in four to find the centre and mark the folds with a hard pencil or fabric pen.

2 Using two strands of crewel wool (yarn), work the rug using continental tent stitch for the design and diagonal tent stitch (page 11) for the background.

3 Working from the chart, overleaf, begin at the centre and work the flowing design of the central area and then fill in the background. Work the Greek key border to finish.

4 To complete your rug refer to page 12 for starching and stretching, and to page 13 for edging and fringing.

Greek styles were very popular in Georgian times. The flowing design of the central area of this rug contrasts with the formal Greek key border that contains it. It would grace a music room in an affluent house or could be the rug that well-to-do ladies sit on to pass a genteel afternoon with a little embroidery in the drawing room.

Stitch count 123 x 95
Finished size 6¾ x 5¼in (17.4 x 13.4cm)
Rug shown larger than actual size

Greek-style Georgian Rug

Appletons
crewel wool

- 696
- 695
- 693
- 922

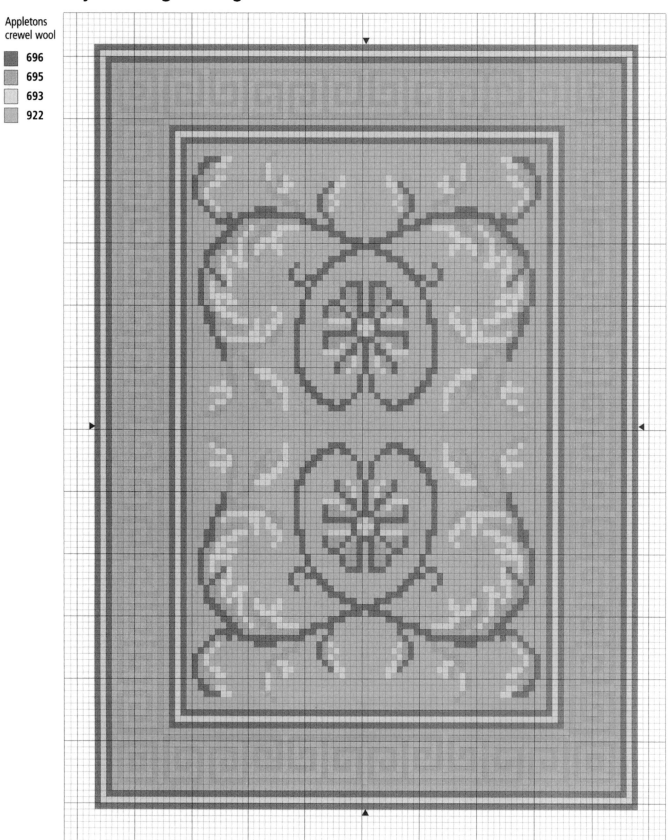

Caucasian Kelim

A kelim or kilim is a pileless woven rug traditionally made in the Middle East and for this design the rich, bright colours that such a rug would have been woven in have been chosen. To make your rug look like an antique version you could imitate faded colours by choosing paler shades. For a really authentic aged look try creating the impression of some worn patches by working areas in one strand of crewel wool (yarn) instead of two.

You will need

14 x 12in (35.4 x 30cm) 18 count interlock canvas

Size 22 tapestry needle

Appletons crewel wool (yarn) as follows:
One skein: green 293; gold 695; mauve 934
Two skeins: blue 925; cream 692
Three skeins: brick red 725

1 Start by binding the edges of the canvas with masking tape to prevent threads snagging. Fold the canvas in four to find the centre and mark the folds with a hard pencil or fabric pen.

2 Using two strands of crewel wool (yarn), work the design from the chart, using continental tent stitch for the design and diagonal tent stitch (page 11) for the brick red background. Begin with the central medallion and go on to work the four smaller medallions.

3 Count carefully out to the first border, stitching this and then the other borders. Finally, stitch the background in brick red.

4 To complete your kelim, refer to page 12 for stretching and to page 13 for edging and fringing.

This miniature rug is a copy of a flat-woven rug made by the Turkish-speaking Shah Savan nomads, who in earlier times wandered over large parts of Azerbaijan and the southern Caucasus. The original was probably made some time in the second half of the 19th century. Oriental or Eastern carpets have been popular ever since the first merchants brought them back from their travels and this design would sit well in several periods, including our own, but would look its best with simple oak furniture.

Caucasian Kelim

Stitch count 139 x 103
Finished size 7¾ x 5¾in (19.5 x 14.5cm)
Kelim shown actual size

Appletons
crewel wool

▮ 925
▮ 293
▮ 695
▯ 692
▮ 725
▮ 934

41

Lattice Rose Stair Carpet

This design is very adaptable as the colours can easily be changed to create very different looks. You could alter the backgrounds to two shades of blue or change all the colours completely. Other pastel shades could be selected or even a much stronger set – bright red roses on a cream background with a navy centre panel and a red trellis perhaps? Here the design is worked as a stair carpet but it would also make a pretty runner in a hallway or landing or just a short length fringed as a rug. It is stitched with four strands of stranded cotton (floss) on 22 count canvas so it is not too thick to fit under stair rods, but if you are not using the design on stairs then use six strands on 18 count canvas. Anchor alternatives are provided.

You will need

6in (15cm) wide x the length of your
stairs plus 6in (15cm) 22 count canvas

Size 24 tapestry needle

DMC stranded cotton (floss) as follows
(Anchor conversions in brackets):
One skein: dark green 3012 (843);
light green 3013 (845);
dark yellow 676 (874);
light yellow 677 (802);
dark coral 3778 (1013);
mid coral 3779 (868);
light coral 948 (1012)

(To make a length longer than
15in (38cm), double up on both
yellow background colours)

1 Bind the edges of the canvas with masking tape to prevent snagging. Fold it in half lengthways to find the centre line and mark the fold with a hard pencil or fabric pen.

2 Start working 3in (7.5cm) from one end of your canvas, using four strands of stranded cotton (floss). For a really smooth finish separate the strands and recombine them to remove the twist. Work the design from the chart using continental tent stitch for the design and diagonal tent stitch (page 11) for the background. Begin with the roses in the outer borders, then work the coral lattice and finally fill in the backgrounds. The chart can be repeated as many times as you like.

3 To complete your stair carpet refer to page 12 for stretching, to page 13 for edging and to page 26 (the introduction to the Oriental stair carpet) for fitting to stairs.

This simple flower border and trellis design is a classical one that will fit well into many period styles or even in a contemporary dolls' house.

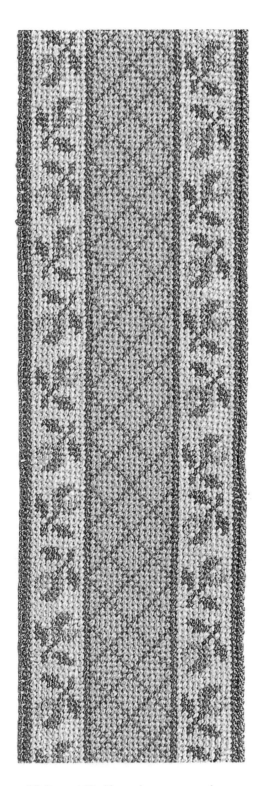

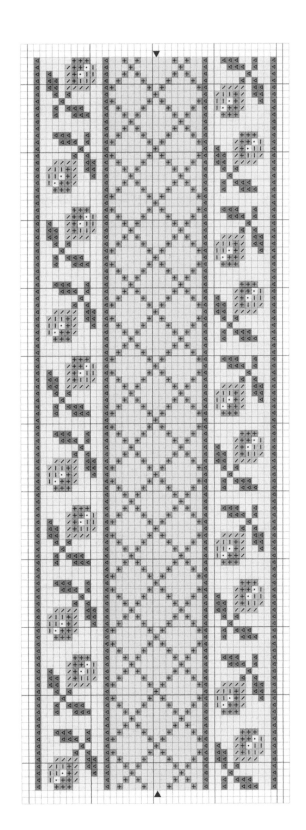

Stitch count 39 wide x as long as you need
Finished size 1¾in (4.5cm) wide
Carpet shown wider than actual size

DMC stranded cotton (Anchor conversions)

+	3778 (1013)
I	3779 (868)
•	948 (1012)
◁	3012 (843)
/	3013 (845)
	676 (874)
	677 (802)

43

Victorian Posy and Trellis Rug

This lovely rug could very easily be made into a square carpet by extending the short sides to the same length as the long ones and then extending the trellis to fill. You could also change the colour of the border to suit your dolls' house décor by picking out one of the shades from the central posy and using that instead. If you do this, you may have to change the colour of the little flowers in the border accordingly.

You will need

13 x 11in (33 x 28cm) 18 count interlock canvas

Size 22 tapestry needle

Appletons crewel wool (yarn) as follows:
One skein: dark coral 205; mid coral 204; light coral 203; rust 207; dark blue 925; mid blue 924; light blue 921; dark green 336; mid green 334; light green 332; yellow 473; light gold 692; mauve 933

1 Begin by binding the edges of the canvas with masking tape to prevent threads snagging. Fold the canvas in four to find the centre and mark the folds with a hard pencil or fabric pen.

2 Using two strands of crewel wool (yarn), work the design from the chart overleaf, using continental tent stitch for the design and diagonal tent stitch (page 11) for the background. Begin with the central posy.

3 Stitch the mauve trellis pattern, counting carefully out to the flower border, and then complete the inner area by working the trellis background in light gold. Work the flower border and the mid coral outer border to finish.

4 Complete your rug by referring to page 12 for starching and stretching and to page 13 for edging and fringing.

The floral posy in the centre of this rug is based on a Victorian Berlin woolwork chart. These were hand painted and produced in vast quantities in Victorian times and featured big, beautifully coloured flowers. Today, these charts are collectors' items and are almost as attractive as the embroideries stitched from them.

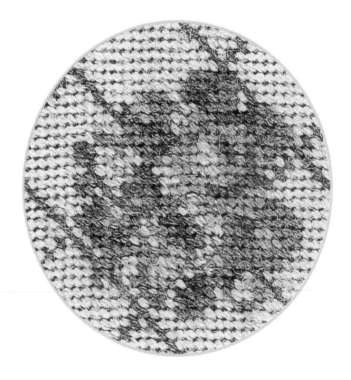

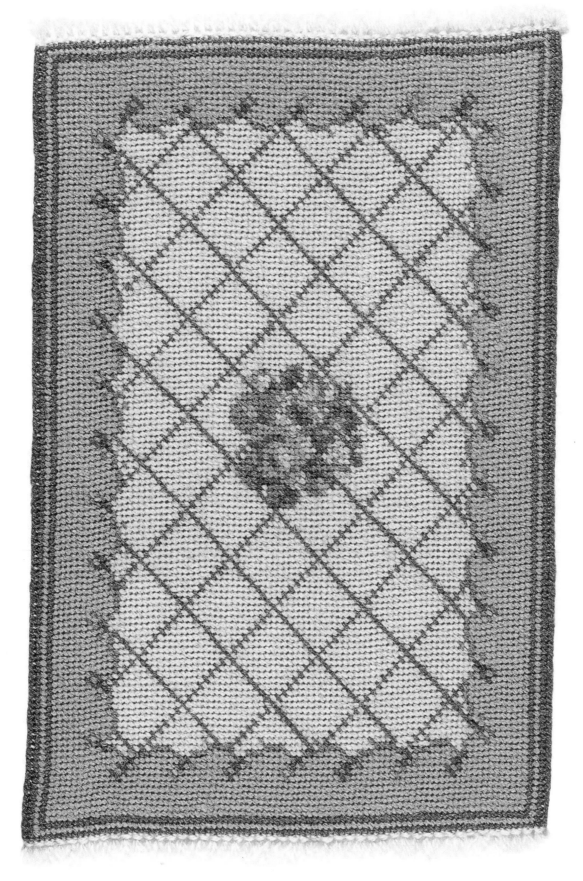

Stitch count 132 x 92
Finished size 7¼ x 5in (18.5 x 13cm)
Rug shown larger than actual size

Victorian Posy and Trellis Rug

Appletons crewel wool

	692
	933
	473
◢	336
	334
●	207
○	205
⊓	204
•	203
	925
△	924
I	921
—	332

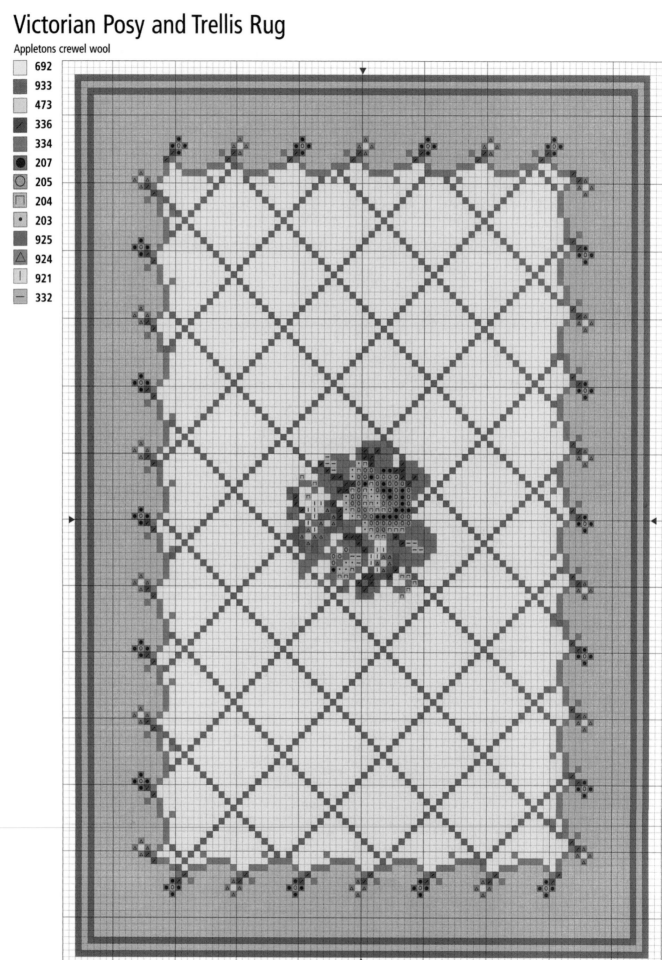

Clarice Cliff Mat

The vivid colours in this mat are the ones used by the ceramic designer Clarice Cliff in 1932. There was a pastel version produced at the same time but examples of it are rare, you could, however, create your own pale version if this is too bright for you. Here it is worked on 24 count canvas with one strand of crewel wool (yarn). To make a bigger rug use two strands on 18 count canvas. The black back stitch outlines are optional but if added after the tent stitch they do make the design more like the original china.

You will need

7 x 6in (18 x 15cm) 24 count canvas

Size 24 tapestry needle

Appletons crewel wool (yarn) as follows:
One skein: mauve 933; dark orange 994; light orange 854; charcoal 998; yellow 474; green 428; blue 322; pale gold 692

Black stranded cotton (floss) for outlines

This bright little mat will cheer up a kitchen doorway or sit by the back door perhaps. It is a copy of a design by Clarice Cliff on her 'Bizarre' range of china. 'Orange Roof Cottage' was introduced in 1932 and is one of the best known of her designs.

1 Start by binding the edges of the canvas with masking tape to prevent snagging. Fold the canvas in four to find the centre and mark the folds with a hard pencil or fabric pen.

2 Using one strand of crewel wool (yarn) work the design from the chart using continental tent stitch for the design and diagonal tent stitch (page 11) for the background. Begin at the centre of the chart.

3 Add the black back stitch outlines using two strands of stranded cotton (floss).

4 Complete the mat by referring to page 12 for stretching and page 13 for edging.

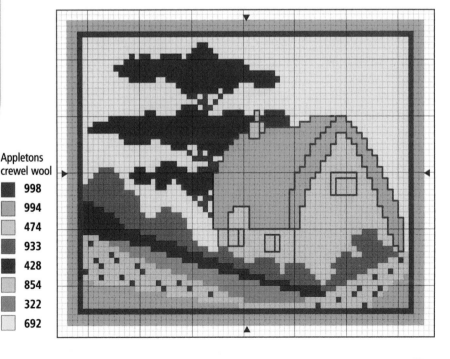

Appletons crewel wool

■	998
▨	994
▨	474
▨	933
■	428
▨	854
▨	322
▨	692

Stitch count 69 x 54
Finished size 2¾ x 2¼in (7.3 x 5.7cm)
Mat shown larger than actual size

Persian Prayer Mat

This attractive little mat is shown worked on 18 count interlock canvas with crewel wool (yarn). Prayer rugs sometimes had a silk pile for more affluent people to kneel on, so try working this design in the Caron silk and wool mixture used for the Oriental Stair Carpet on page 26 on a 26 count linen. It will be small but very beautiful!

You will need

8 x 7in (20 x 18cm) 18 count interlock canvas

Size 22 tapestry needle

Appletons crewel wool (yarn) as follows:
One skein: mauve 934; dark rust 207; light rust 205; gold 695; blue 925

Prayer mats have been hand woven for centuries in Persia (now Iran). The mat is laid on the floor of the mosque so that the arrow shape points in the direction of Mecca during prayer. These small mats will sit happily alongside most period styles and make lovely occasional rugs throughout a dolls' house.

Stitch count 73 x 47
Finished size 4⅛ x 2⅝in (10.3 x 6.6cm)
Mat shown larger than actual size

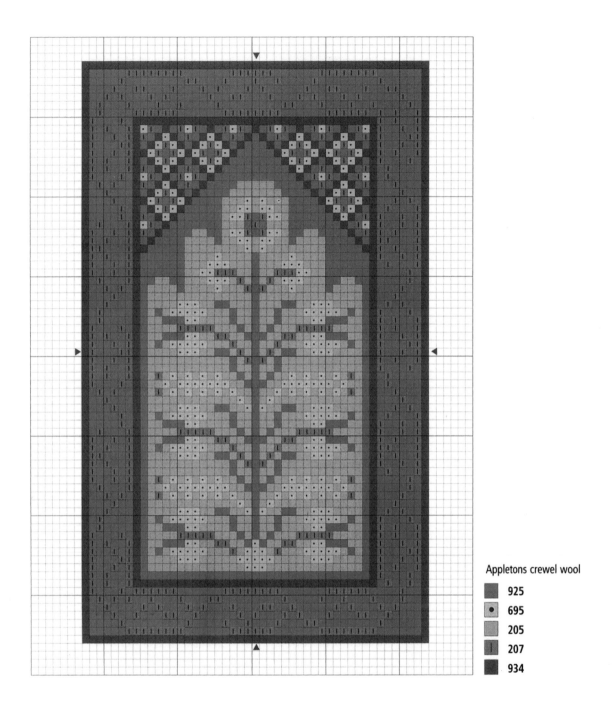

Appletons crewel wool

■	925
•	695
▫	205
▌	207
■	934

1 Start by binding the edges of the canvas with masking tape to prevent threads snagging. Fold the canvas in four to find the centre and mark the folds with a hard pencil or fabric pen.

2 Using two strands of crewel wool (yarn), work the design from the chart using continental tent stitch for the design and diagonal tent stitch (page 11) for the background. Begin stitching from the centre of the chart and the centre of the canvas.

3 To complete you mat refer to page 12 for starching and stretching and to page 13 for edging and fringing.

49

Sunflower Rag Rug

Plaiting, pegging and hooking are all traditional methods of making mats and rugs from rags. You will need to collect scraps of very fine fabric to make this hooked rag rug – the Liberty Tana Lawn that has been used for this one is ideal. There are four colour groups: plain fabrics give a stronger colour, like the green leaves here, while prints produce a more interesting effect. You might like to practise on a spare piece of linen to see how your colours work. Natural 28 count linen has been used as the backing instead of the hessian that would be used on a full-sized rug. This little rug is a bit fiddly to make but the end result is so sweet that it is well worth the effort.

You will need

6 x 6in (15 x 15cm) natural
28 count linen

Closely woven cotton lawn cut into long strips ¼in (0.5cm) wide in four colours: green, yellow, brown and deep blue

Size 1.00mm crochet hook

Tracing paper

Fine black felt-tipped pen

Sewing thread

1 Trace the sunflower design given here on to a sheet of tracing paper with a black pen. Tape this tracing to a window and then tape the piece of linen over the tracing and draw the design on to the fabric using a black felt-tipped pen. Alternatively, trace the drawing using a light source under a sheet of glass.

This little mat is made like a Proddy rug from Norfolk, England. These were backed with hessian and the pile was made from strips of old fabric. Old clothes or curtains were cut into strips and then hooked or 'prodded' through the hessian with a latch hook. By grouping the strips in colours a pattern was created: some were quite complicated and others, made by children, much simpler.

Finished size 2½ x 2in (6.3 x 5cm)
Rug shown larger than actual size

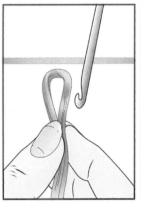 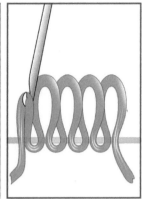

2 It is easier to make this rug if the fabric is held taut in an embroidery hoop. Begin in the centre of the flower using brown fabric. Push the crochet hook through the linen, place a loop of fabric over the hook and pull it up through the fabric. Repeat this just next to the first loop (see diagrams above).

Take care not to pull out loops as you make another – as work progresses and the loops become tightly packed they will not pull out so easily. Pack the loops very tightly so that they all stay in.

As you come to the end of a strip just start another, leaving about 1in (2.5cm) hanging below. Take care that these ends do not get caught up in the loops – you can trim them as you go.

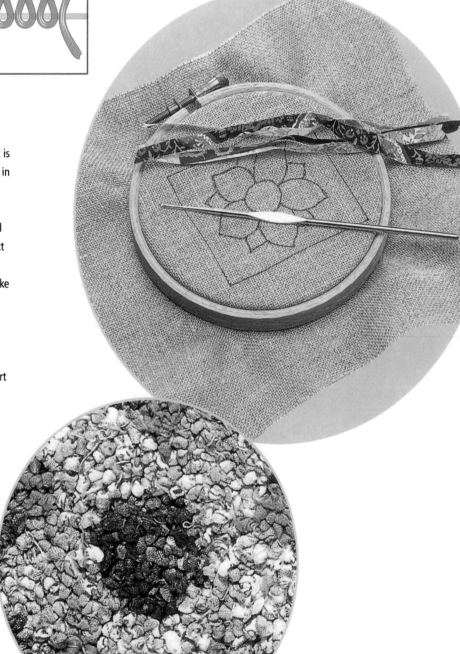

3 Once you have filled the central brown circle fill the petals with yellow strips and then the leaves in green. Finally, fill all the background in blue. Trim any ends of the fabric strips to about ¼in (0.5cm) Trim the edge of the linen ½in (1.25cm) from the loops. Apply Fray Check to the edges and allow it to dry. Trim the corners and finish the rug by folding in all the edges and fixing them down with ordinary sewing thread and herringbone stitch (page 11) on the back of the rug.

Laceby Tiles

The central area of this rug is a repeating pattern so you could make a much bigger one with a square centre panel or make it narrower and longer to create a runner for a hallway or landing or even a stair carpet. The colours used are warm earth tones combined with a rich red and quite a strong blue.

You will need

13 x 11in (33 x 28cm) 18 count interlock canvas

Size 22 tapestry needle

Appletons crewel wool (yarn) as follows:
One skein: cream 882; beige 692; red 725; blue 323; charcoal 998; gold 695
Two skeins: brown 911

1 Start by binding the edges of the canvas with masking tape to prevent threads snagging. Fold the canvas in four to find the centre and mark the folds with a hard pencil or fabric pen.

2 Using two strands of crewel wool (yarn), work the design from the centre of the chart overleaf and the centre of the canvas, using continental tent stitch for the design and diagonal tent stitch (page 11) for the background. Count the precise shapes carefully so that they fit together exactly, working the central area followed by the border.

3 Complete your rug by referring to page 12 for starching and stretching and to page 13 for edging and fringing.

This striking design is based on a beautiful Victorian tiled hallway at Laceby Manor in Lincolnshire, England. Many Victorian houses still have their tiled halls and porches and if used in the hall of your dolls' house on a plain, dark floor this rug will give the impression of these characteristic tiles.

Stitch count 123 x 79
Finished size 6¾ x 4⅜in (17.4 x 11.1cm)
Rug shown larger than actual size

Laceby Tiles

Appletons
crewel wool

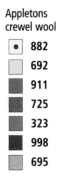

- 882
- 692
- 911
- 725
- 323
- 998
- 695

Chinese Dragon Rug

Chinese rugs are often woven in silk so stranded cotton (floss) has been used to give this rug a sheen. As the pile on these rugs is usually fine and close, here a fine canvas has been stitched with four strands of cotton but if this does not suit your eyesight you can substitute an 18 count canvas and use six strands instead. Stranded cotton (floss) has a twist in the strands but to achieve a really smooth effect it is well worth taking the strands apart and recombining them to remove this twist. In this way all the strands lie parallel and the shine on the thread will be more evident. It is up to you whether you do this but don't give up halfway though the rug as you will notice the difference!

Two charts are provided for this rug, with instructions for stitching the red and jade version. The chart for the blue and gold dragon is the same as the red and jade one, with just the colours changed to give a strikingly different effect – choose the version that best suits your dolls' house.

You will need

12 x 10in (30 x 25cm) 22 count canvas

Size 24 tapestry needle

DMC stranded cotton (floss) as follows
(blue/gold colourway in brackets):
One skein: brick red 3777 (dark blue 820);
orange 900 (light blue 799);
cream 3047 (gold 783);
dark jade 500 (mid blue 797);
dark brown 3371 (dark brown 3371)
Three skeins: light jade 991 (cream 746)

(Note: Anchor thread conversions are in
brackets with the chart keys)

In China, the dragon represents the union of earthly and celestial forces. This one, clutching a pearl in each claw, symbolizes his function as guardian of the moon. Anything Chinese was very sought after for interior design in Britain at the beginning of the 19th century and this rug could be complemented by lacquered furniture and ceramic ginger jars in a hallway or be placed in a corner of a formal drawing room.

1 Bind the edges of the canvas with masking tape to prevent snagging. Fold the canvas in four to find the centre and mark the folds with a hard pencil or fabric pen.

2 Using four strands of stranded cotton (floss), work the design from the chart, using continental tent stitch for the design and diagonal tent stitch (page 11) for the background. Begin at the centre, working the dragon first.

3 Count carefully out to the border and stitch this in brick red, and then finish your stitching by working the light jade background.

4 Complete your rug by referring to page 12 for starching and stretching and to page 13 for edging and fringing.

Red and jade dragon:
Stitch count 129 x 89
Finished size 5¾ x 4in (15 x 10cm)
Rug shown actual size

Chinese Dragon Rug

DMC stranded cotton
(Anchor conversions)

- 3777 (1015)
- 900 (326)
- 3047 (956)
- 500 (683)
- 991 (1076)
- 3371 (382)

Blue and gold dragon:
Stitch count 129 x 89
Finished size 5¾ x 4in (15 x 10cm)

Alternative colourway
DMC stranded cotton
(Anchor conversions)

- 820 (134)
- 799 (136)
- 783 (306)
- 797 (139)
- 746 (386)
- 3371 (382)

57

Embroidered Felt Numnah

This little rug is embroidered on a piece of handmade felt, though felt from a craft shop is fine too. If commercial felt seems a bit smooth, rough it up a bit with a wire brush before you start. Medici wool (yarn) is ideal for this project because it is very fine and it is easy to change the colour scheme to use up any bits you may have. This rug would make a lovely bedside rug but if the shape was altered it would also suit other places in a dolls' house.

You will need

7 x 5in (18 x 12.5cm) cream felt

Size 7 crewel needle

Tracing paper

Fine black felt-tipped pen

Vanishing embroidery marker

DMC Medici wool (yarn) as follows:
One skein: mauve 8123; dark red 8100;
gold 8302; yellow 8326; green 8407;
pink 8139; dark blue 8930;
light blue 8931

1 Trace the drawing provided below on to a sheet of tracing paper with a black felt-tipped pen. Tape the tracing to a window and then tape the piece of felt over the tracing – you should be able to see the design through the cream felt. Draw the design on to the felt using a vanishing embroidery marker or a water-soluble pen. (If you are working at night or on a very dull day use a blank page on a computer screen instead of a window, or a light under a sheet of glass as the light source to help with the tracing.)

2 Using one strand of Medici wool (yarn) work the design in chain stitch (page 11) referring to the picture for the colours.

3 Trim the edge of the felt to ⅜in (1cm) away from the stitching. To finish, use a wire brush (a small one meant for suede shoes is ideal) to rough up the edges.

In the past, thick felt made from sheep's wool was used as a pad under horse saddles in the Middle East and probably still is. As with many utilitarian items made from fabric it was not long before they were embellished with embroidery. These beautiful pieces then become collectable, their original use almost forgotten when they were sought as decorative objects.

Finished size 5¾ x 3¾in (14.5 x 9.5cm)
Rug shown larger than actual size

Art Deco Rug

This Art Deco rug is worked in the colours of the period and is a copy of an original by Betty Joel, a designer in the 1930s who specialized in signed rugs and luxury furniture with large, rounded curves. The orange in the rug has a tweed effect created by mixing two colours in the needle – this breaks up the solid colours and brings the design to life.

You will need

13 x 10in (33 x 25cm) 18 count interlock canvas

Size 22 tapestry needle

Appletons crewel wool (yarn) as follows:
One skein: deep plum 934; orange 695/765; brown 764; beige 762; cream 882; pale gold 692

1 Start by binding the edges of the canvas with masking tape to prevent threads snagging. Fold the canvas in four to find the centre and mark the folds with a hard pencil or fabric pen.

2 Using two strands of crewel wool (yarn), work the design from the chart, using continental tent stitch for the design and diagonal tent stitch (page 11) for the background. Begin at the centre of the chart and canvas and count the shapes carefully so that they fit together exactly. Work the orange sections with one strand each of 695 and 765 in the needle.

3 To complete your rug, refer to page 12 for stretching and page 13 for edging.

Stitch count 127 x 69
Finished size 7⅛ x 3¾in (17.9 x 9.7cm)
Rug shown smaller than actual size

The 1920s saw a great change in design; shapes were geometric but flowing and colours were predominantly soft browns, creams and beige. A rug was part of a furnishing scheme and would be chosen as if it were a piece of art, which indeed it is. This rug would be ideal if you are planning a modernist room within your dolls' house.

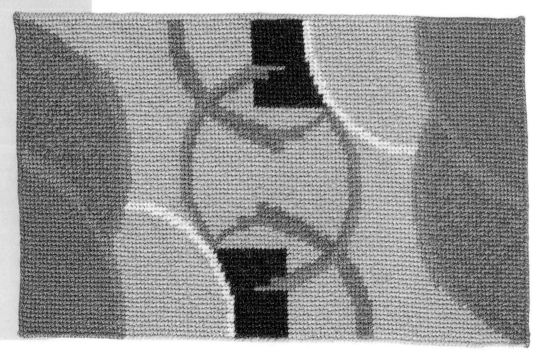

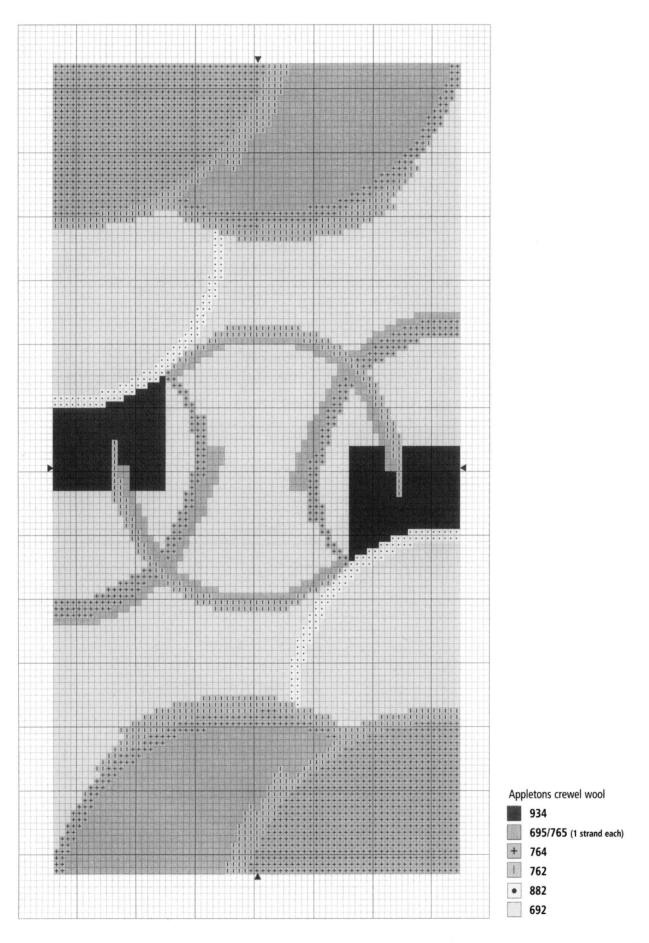

Appletons crewel wool

◼	**934**
▦	**695/765** (1 strand each)
+	**764**
|	**762**
•	**882**
▢	**692**

Suppliers

Appletons Bros Ltd
Thames Works, Church Street, Chiswick,
London WE 2PE, UK
tel: 0181 994 0711
For tapestry wools

Burford Needlecraft Centre
117 High Street, Burford,
Oxon. OX18 4RG, UK
tel: 01993 822136
www.needlework.co.uk
Mail order for threads and canvases

Caron Threads
Macleod Craft Marketing, West Yonderton,
Warlock Road, Bridge of Weir,
Renfrewshire, PA11 3SR, Scotland
tel: 01505 612618
For Caron threads

Coats Crafts UK
PO Box 22, Lingfield Estate, McMullen Road,
Darlington, County Durham, DL1 1YQ, UK
tel: 01325 365457 (for a list of stockists)
For a wide range of needlework supplies,
including Anchor threads

DMC Creative World Ltd
Pullman Road, Wigston,
Leicestershire LE18 2DY, UK
tel: 0116 281 1040
fax: 0116 281 3592
www.dmc/cw.com
For a full range of needlework supplies, including threads
and Zweigart fabrics

Dolls' House Emporium
Write or telephone for your free colour catalogue of
the complete range quoting EDC1:
EDC1, Ripley,
Derbyshire, DE5 3YD, UK
tel: 01773 514400
www.dollshouse.com

Jojays
Moore Road, Bourton-on-the-Water,
Gloucestershire GL54 2AZ, UK
tel: 01451 810081
www.jojays.co.uk
www.jojays.com
Dolls' houses and miniatures specialist shop that stocks the
staircases used in this book and just about everything else
for the dolls' house

Needleworks by Sue Hawkins
East Wing, Highfield House, School Lane,
Whitminster, Gloucestershire GL2 7PJ, UK
Sue Hawkins' company supplies counted canvaswork,
crewelwork and cross stitch kits as well as upholstered
embroidery frames. For a catalogue write (enclosing a
stamped addressed envelope) or telephone 01452 740118

The Viking Loom
22 High Petergate, York,
North Yorkshire YO1 2EH, UK
tel: 01904 620587
www.vikingloom.co.uk
Plus mail order for threads and canvas

Zweigart/Joan Toggit Ltd
262 Old Brunswick Road, Suite E, Picataway,
NJ 08854-3756, USA
tel: 732 562 8888
www.zweigart.com
For embroidery fabrics and general supplies

Acknowledgments

My thanks to John for being there (and to Hannah and Jo for not being there); to Cheryl Brown at David & Charles for believing in me; to Lin Clements for editing with such care; to the ladies who helped me with the stitching, they are – Mary Bridgewater, Olwyn Peters, Lesley Clegg and Caroline Gibbons; to Beryl and Steve Lee of Laceby Manor for allowing me to use their floor (for the design and for sleeping on!); to Zweigart for supplies of fine canvas; to the International Feltmakers' Association for the piece of handmade felt for my embroidered rug and last, as always, to my two spaniels Billy and Tommy, who keep me company as I work and agree with my every word!

About the author

Sue Hawkins began her career working for an antique dealer, restoring seventeenth-century English embroidery. Her knowledge of the needlework business was gained whilst owning and running an embroidery shop for several years, and since 1991 she has designed for and run her own successful kit-manufacturing company, Needleworks (see Suppliers). Sue also teaches embroidery workshops at her home and around the country. Many of the workshops are run on behalf of the Cross Stitch Guild, of which she is technical director. This is her fifth book for David & Charles. Sue lives near Stroud, Gloucestershire, UK.

Index

Printed in Great Britain
by Amazon.co.uk, Ltd.,
Marston Gate.